W9-AYR-794

Mr. Olney
Librarian

Starting the Day

James Olney works in a library. He is an **information specialist** (IN-fer-MAY-shun SPESH-uh-list), or librarian. This means his specialty is helping **patrons** (PAY-trinz) find answers to their questions. He began working at his library when he was only fourteen years old. He was a **page** (PAYJ), or a librarian's helper. He loved working in the library so much that he went to college to earn a **degree** (duh-GREE) in library science. He says there was never anything else he wanted to be. Now when he comes to work each day, the pages help him.

◀ James Olney looks forward to coming to work every day.

Detective Work

James spends some time each day at the **reference** (REF-er-ens) desk answering the phone. Children and adults call the library with all kinds of questions. One girl wants to find an answer for a school project. James will help her find the answer. James works like a **detective** (dih-TEK-tiv). Both librarians and detectives **research** (REE-serch) information in books and magazines or on computers. "Librarians don't have to know the answer," says James. "We just have to know how to help people find it."

Computers and phones allow James to help patrons who can't get to the library. ▶

"I'm Looking for a Book"

People also come to the library to ask James about books. A woman asks him for help. "I'm looking for a book," she says. "I know the title and the author, but I don't know where to find it." James shows her how books can be found easily in the **card catalog** (KARD KAT-uh-log) on the computer. James finds out that the book is not in his library. But he can get it for her from a different library that has the book. She will only have to wait a day or two.

◄ Teaching people how to find information is James's specialty.

Walking the Floor

James takes some time out of each day to be a floor walker. He walks around the library asking if anyone needs help. People need help with many things. Someone may want to know where to find a certain magazine. Someone else may want to know where the children's books are kept. Sometimes patrons need help with the machines. Today, a man is having trouble with one of the computers. He says, "Can you help me save something on a disk?" James teaches him what to do.

Sometimes people come to James with tough questions. Other times people have questions that are easy to ▶ answer. But they are all important to James.

Homework Help

Some girls are working on a project for school. James asks them if they need help. One girl asks if he can explain what something in her library book means. James shows her where she can look in her book to find the answer. Librarians help students in many ways. This library even has a special homework shelf. Teachers at local schools tell James what books students will need for their homework, and he sets them aside so students can find them quickly.

◀ James doesn't give students answers to their homework. But he will tell them in which books they can find more information.

Weeding the Books

One of James's jobs is to weed through the math and science books. This means he picks out books that may be falling apart or that have information in them that is old or no longer true. It is a little bit like weeding a garden. Just as weeding a garden makes room for new plants, James makes room for new books. Uh, oh! The glue on the spine of this book has dried out. All of the pages are falling out! Sometimes James is able to fix a book, but this one will have to be **recycled** (ree-SY-kuld).

◄ James makes sure the books on his shelves are in good shape and contain the most up-to-date information.

An Elevator Ride for Books

When he has pulled out the old books, James loads them onto a cart. He pushes the cart to a small elevator called a **dumbwaiter** (DUM-way-ter). "The books are too heavy to carry down the stairs," he says. Instead, the books travel by themselves on the tiny elevator until they reach the first floor. Later, James will take them off the dumbwaiter and place them in the recycling bin. He will order new books to take their places on the bookshelves.

Most libraries have dumbwaiters, ▶ like the one James uses.

On the Web

Librarians have to know a lot about computers. In fact, James is his library's Internet wizard. He is the person everyone comes to with questions about the Internet. Even other librarians come to him for help. James **designed** (dih-ZYND) a Web site for his library. Patrons can click onto the site from their home computers. They can find out about library programs or if a book they wish to borrow is at the library. He also teaches classes at the library for people who want to learn more about the Internet and want to design their own Web sites.

◀ James uses his computer skills to help patrons find information on the World Wide Web.

A Fun Day

At the end of the day, there are books, magazines, and newspapers to return to the shelves. The machines will be turned off and the library will be empty and quiet. James thinks a library is a fun place to work. What he likes most about being a librarian is that he learns new things every day. Each time he helps a patron or answers a question, he learns something new. "I love my job," he says, with a smile.

Web Sites:

You can visit the Web site that James designed and learn more about his library at:

http://www.suffolk.lib.ny.us/libraries/netwalk

GLOSSARY

card catalog (KARD KAT-uh-log) An alphabetical list of items in a library that are stored in a cabinet or on a computer.

CD-ROM (SEE-dee RAHM) A compact disc with information on it that can only be read by a computer or a CD player.

degree (duh-GREE) A certificate saying that you've finished a course of study.

design (dih-ZYN) To plan the form and structure of something.

detective (dih-TEK-tiv) A person who searches for the facts about something.

dumbwaiter (DUM-way-ter) A small elevator used for moving books.

information specialist (IN-fer-MAY-shun SPESH-uh-list) Someone who is an expert in finding and organizing facts.

microfilm (MY-kroh-film) A kind of film used to make small photographs of pages from a newspaper or magazine that can be read on a special machine.

page (PAYJ) A young adult who assists librarians.

patron (PAY-trin) A regular customer.

recycle (ree-SY-kul) To use something again in a different way.

reference (REF-er-ens) Having to do with getting or giving information.

research (REE-serch) To study carefully something to find out more about it.

Index